W9-CLU-385

CRICKETOLOGY

CRICKETOLOGY

South Huntington Pub. Lib.
145 Pidgeon Hill Rd.
Huntington Sta., N.Y. 11746

by Michael Elsohn Ross

photographs by Brian Grogan • illustrations by Darren Erickson

 Carolrhoda Books, Inc. / Minneapolis

595.726
Rosenberg

To my father, who passed on his love of crickety summer nights.

Without the creativity and enthusiasm of the second- through sixth-grade students of El Portal Elementary and the support of their teachers, Carl Brownless and Phyllis Weber, this book would not have been possible. The author would also like to thank the students of Vista de Valle School in Claremont, California, and Tom Jones and his students at Alicia Reyes School in Merced, California, for their assistance.

Text copyright © 1996 by Michael Elsohn Ross
Photographs copyright © 1996 by Brian Grogan
Illustrations copyright © 1996 by Carolrhoda Books, Inc.

All rights reserved. International copyright secured. No part of this book may be reproduced, stored in a retrieval system, or transmitted in any form or by any means—electronic, mechanical, photocopying, recording, or otherwise—without the prior written permission of Carolrhoda Books, Inc., except for the inclusion of brief quotations in an acknowledged review.

This book is available in two editions:
Library binding by Carolrhoda Books, Inc.,
    a division of Lerner Publishing Group
Soft cover by First Avenue Editions,
    an imprint of Lerner Publishing Group
241 First Avenue North, Minneapolis, MN 55401 U.S.A.

Website address: www.lernerbooks.com

Library of Congress Cataloging-in-Publications Data

Ross, Michael Elsohn, 1952–
    Cricketology / by Michael Elsohn Ross ; photographs by Brian Grogan ; illustrations by
Darren Erickson.
        p.   cm. — (Backyard buddies)
    Includes index.
    Summary: Provides instructions for finding, collecting, and keeping crickets and suggests
how to delve into the secret lives of these chirping neighbors.
        ISBN: 0-87614-985-9 (lib. bdg. : alk. paper)
        ISBN: 0-87614-900-x (pbk. : alk. paper)
        1. Crickets — Juvenile literature. 2. Crickets — Experiments — Juvenile literature.
3. Crickets as pets — Juvenile literature. [1. Crickets as pets. 2. Crickets — Experiments.
3. Experiments.] I. Grogan, Brian, ill. II. Erickson, Darren, ill. III. Title. IV. Series: Ross,
Michael Elsohn, Backyard buddies.
    QL508.G8R67   1995
    595.7'26 — dc20   95-4559

Manufactured in the United States of America
3 4 5 6 7 8 – JR – 06 05 04 03 02 01

Contents

Listen with your legs,

Talk with your wings;

Be still as a cricket

As the night air sings.

Crick-et! Crick-et! Crick-et! You have probably heard crickets singing before, but have you ever really gotten to know one? Hidden in backyard tangles and secret retreats, these lively jumpers lead lives as strange as any punk rocker.

Yet unlike the way some people see rock musicians, many folks think of crickets as peaceful songsters. Other people may think of them as mere fish food, and some might even react to a jumping cricket with a fearful "eek!"

There's no need to fear crickets, though. They don't bite, sting, or eat humans. Since we are giants compared to them, we are more likely to harm them—unless we are truly gentle.

Can you imagine yourself as a giant cricketologist? A mammologist studies mammals, while a cricketologist investigates crickets. To be an offical one, all you need is an interest in getting to know your chirping, hopping, long-legged neighbors.

Finding a cricket when it is singing can be a comic event. Though you may creep up as stealthily as a cat, somehow the cricket senses your approach and shuts up as tight as a slammed door. Without the chirps to guide you, further searching is hopeless. Fooled by a little bug, you must wait until it starts to sing once again. With time and patience, it *is* possible to spy on singing crickets—but if you just want to catch a cricket, a general inspection of backyard hiding places will do. Look under rocks, logs, or other possible shelters, and you may discover crickets at rest.

Going on a Cricket Hunt

All you need for collecting crickets are some lightning-fast reflexes and a plastic jar with small holes in the lid. Crickets are speedy hoppers and scramblers. After turning over rocks or other shelters, be ready to reach out rapidly to trap a cricket under your paw. Next, use your other hand to gently transfer it to the jar. Remember, crickets are harmless, so there is no need to worry about holding them. When left in the sun, a clear jar heats up quickly—like a miniature greenhouse. Be sure to keep the jar in the shade so your cricket won't get toasted. If you can't find any crickets outdoors, you may be able to buy some at a local bait or pet shop.

In Japan and China, it is common for children to bring crickets home as pets. In fact, parents often buy their kids special cricket cages. If you don't live in one of these countries, consider how your folks might react to a cricket as a guest in your household. If they get upset by crawly critters, you might want to show them this article from the highly respected make-believe newspaper, *The Times Mirror Chronicle Gazette*.

The Perfect Pet

Young Gilbert and Hilda Filbert, of Griffin, Georgia, finally resolved their family's pet dilemma in a most daring manner. After giving away a puppy that ate Mr. Filbert's shoes, losing a gerbil in the laundry room, and returning a foul mouthed parrot to the pet store, the Filbert family was pet-less.

Saddened, to say the least, Gilbert and Hilda searched for the perfect pet. While moving an old tire in the backyard, they discovered a most handsome cricket. They convinced their parents to let them keep their new friend for a little while as a guest. Though having a bug as a pet seemed a bit odd, Ma and Pa Filbert remembered Jiminy Cricket. "If it was good enough for Pinocchio and Geppetto, it's good enough for me," Mr. Filbert announced to the kids, who now sit around in the evenings listening to their talented visitor. Mr. Filbert adds, "My shoes are safe, my kids' ears are safe, and best of all, the cricket seems happy too!"

Royal Homes

Over a thousand years ago, before the days of tape cassettes and compact disc players, Chinese royalty listened to crickets singing in golden cages. Peasants, who couldn't afford gold, housed their crickets in cages made of bamboo or clay. In the thirteenth century, the *Tsu Chi King (Book of Crickets)* was written to advise people on cricket care.

To keep crickets in your home, you need neither cages of gold nor bamboo. A large plastic jar with holes poked in the lid will do just fine. Cover the bottom of the jar with a one-inch layer of moist soil and add a rock or small block of wood for your crickets to burrow under. A few lettuce leaves make a nice cricket meal. Crickets will also munch dog or cat food, but if they start barking or meowing, they have probably eaten too much!

Be sure to keep the jar out of direct sunlight. And a sign announcing "Cricket Castle" will alert the other members of your household that there are insect guests in your home. Enjoy your visitors, but remember, like all guests they should be allowed to return to their own homes after you've had a chance to get to know them better.

Jumping Jars

Most folks don't get too excited about watching a jar of mayonnaise or peanut butter, but spying on a jar of crickets can be more entertaining than reading a cereal box. You can watch your crickets while you eat breakfast or even while you brush your teeth. You can check them out at night with a flashlight. If you keep them next to your bed, you can listen to them all night instead of sleeping—or maybe they can help put you to sleep. Whenever you are in need of fresh entertainment, just check out the activities of your miniature guests.

Do they munch up the meals you provide for them? Do they make a mess in the castle? When your crickets leave droppings and leftover snacks, be a hospitable host and clean out their rooms. Provide them with fresh goodies each day and see if you can find out what they like best. By spying on your crickets, perhaps you can figure out their habits and learn how to keep them happy and healthy. On the other hand, they might learn about you too. Do you think they are watching you?

Life in a jar, even for an animal as small as a cricket, can get a bit cramped. Like kids, they need some space to jump around in. With a little creativity, it's easy to construct a field where crickets can get exercise, fresh air, and some quality playtime.

Cricket Field

Release a cricket inside the tub and watch where it goes. Does it seem interested in any of the objects? Does it stay at one piece of equipment longer than at another?

Slowly move closer to the tub while keeping your eye on the cricket. Does it seem to notice you? How can you tell? Try to touch it. What happens? Can you get it to crawl onto your hand?

What do you think the cricket will do if you put another cricket in the tub? Add a cricket and see what happens. When the crickets have had enough exercise time, don't forget to return them to their castle. They'll be more secure there than hopping down the hall.

You will need:

✓ a deep plastic dishtub (with sides at least six inches high)
✓ a handful of soil or sand
✓ a small container of water
✓ a handful of fresh leaves
✓ a toilet paper tube
✓ toys such as balls, blocks, or minicars
✓ any other items you can think of

Arrange the items listed above however you wish inside the tub. For example, you could leave the sand in one big pile or spread it evenly over the floor of the tub.

Are you aware? Would you notice if your mom shaved her head or if your dad wore high heels? Would you realize it if your best friend got braces? Do you notice small details? Whatever your answers, the Aware Dare is for you. If you are already totally aware, this game will allow you to show off your sharp wits. On the other hand, if you are completely out to lunch, this game will help you tune in to minute details. Being tuned in is extremely helpful when you are becoming familiar with new friends such as crickets. Though it can be played alone, the Aware Dare is a greater challenge with two or more players.

How to Play:

1. Place a cricket in the plastic cup along with the lettuce or pet food.

2. Decide on the order of play.

3. Beginning with player number one, take turns examining the cricket and sharing observations. For example, "It's black," or "It turns its head." Any detail is okay, but no repeats are allowed.

Optional: Pick one player to write down what each of you notices.

4. Continue taking turns in the same order until only one player is able to make a new observation. The last person to share a cricket characteristic is the most aware.

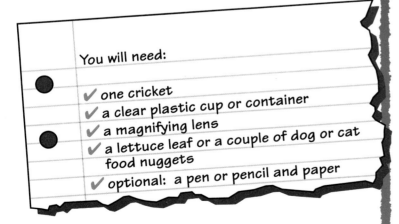

You will need:

✔ one cricket
✔ a clear plastic cup or container
✔ a magnifying lens
✔ a lettuce leaf or a couple of dog or cat food nuggets
✔ optional: a pen or pencil and paper

Have you ever built a model airplane or dollhouse? Do you remember all the different parts you needed to put together? If you were going to make a model of a cricket, would you know what parts to include? Would it need eight legs and five eyes? Would only the legs move or would other parts be flexible too? The items listed below can help you discover what a model of a cricket would look like.

Release the cricket or crickets into the dishtub and use the tools and materials listed to find answers to some cricket questions.

Parts: How many different parts do you notice? What do they look like? Do you see eyebrows, chins, or elbows? Do the parts come in a variety of shapes? How many shapes can you see?

Colors: Some crickets look all black or brown at first glance. Are there any hidden colors? Take a good look and count the number of colors that you can see.

Speed: How fast are crickets? Set crickets one at a time in the middle of a sheet of paper inside the dishtub and record the time it takes each of them to walk or hop off the paper. Do all the crickets move in the same way?

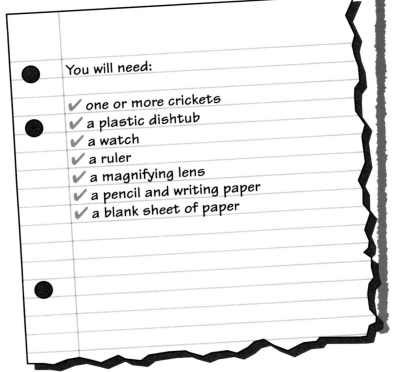

You will need:

✔ one or more crickets
✔ a plastic dishtub
✔ a watch
✔ a ruler
✔ a magnifying lens
✔ a pencil and writing paper
✔ a blank sheet of paper

Even though crickets have been thought of as fine songsters since the days of cave people, no albums, compact discs, or cassettes have been released featuring their most popular hits. Can you picture a famous cricket singer performing on TV? Can you think of what its stage name or the name of its backup band might be? Imagine what the cover art would look like for its award-winning CD. Would you like to make a picture for an imaginary cricket CD? Here's your chance!

You will need:

✓ a cricket
✓ a magnifying lens
✓ a pencil or pen
✓ colored markers or pencils
✓ blank paper

What to Do:

Before you do your final cover, it may help to make some quick sketches of your star cricket, just as a professional artist would do. If your cricket is too active to easily watch, check out page 37 to get ideas on how to slow it down.

1. Walk Your Eyes: A fun way to look closely at a cricket is to pretend that your eyes are two tiny ants. While you peer through a magnifying lens, imagine that your eyes are walking over and under every section of the cricket. (Walk up the legs, over the wings, everywhere.)

2. Warm up Your Fingers: Each time your ant eyes reach a new body part, make a quick sketch of it. These sketches limber up your hand and mind, preparing you for the final cover art.

3. Notice Your Curiosity: If questions such as "What is this thing called?" come up in your brain, jot them down next to your drawings. These questions may be useful in future expeditions.

4. Almost There . . . : Before plunging in to the finished art, you may find it helpful to polish off a few rough sketches of the basic shape and outline of your model.

5. Work Big: It's easier to include small details when you make your artwork big. Give your cover plenty of room.

6. Public Service: If you are feeling generous, donate your art to the local recording studio or to the family fridge.

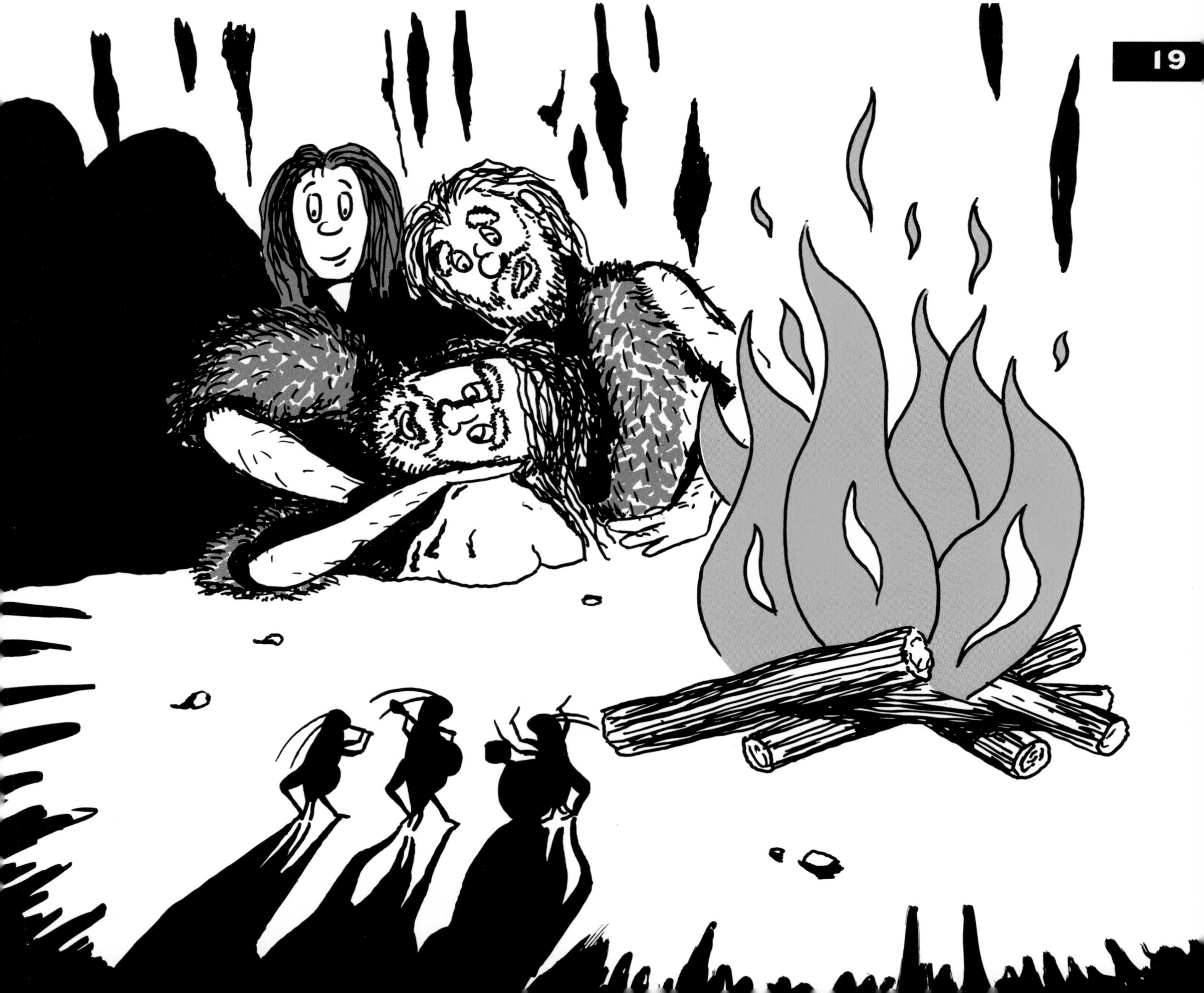

Wondertime

Do you wonder about the secret lives of crickets? Some kids in my town did! Check out their questions.

Do they have wings? If they do, can they fly?

What are the things on their butts? What are the pincers next to their mouths? Are the spikes on their legs hair?

Do crickets like the dark? What happens when crickets get cold?

Can crickets hear? Do they have ears? Do they have noses?

Do they chirp only when it's dark? What do they eat?

Why do they each have a red dot on their foreheads? Why are their back legs yellow underneath? Why are some crickets black?

Why do crickets rest together?

Can crickets climb? Can they climb straight up?

Will a cricket go into water? Can crickets swim?

Can they turn their heads separately from their bodies?

How far can crickets jump? How big do crickets get?

Do you have any answers or any questions of your own? If you have questions, don't let them escape! Simple questions have launched many a wild expedition. Think of the journeys started by questions such as, "How deep is the sea?" or "How far does this river go?" Jot down some cricket questions for fun. Who knows where they might lead you!

Follow That Question

Are you ready to track the unknown? Are you prepared to plunge into mysteries? If you are, all you need to do is grab hold of a crickety question. Is there something you really wonder about crickets? Yes? Well, let that question lead you on a journey. Below are some tips for curious cricketologists.

—Experiment: You can always chase a question by experimenting. The section on page 37 called Kid Experiments has stories about experiments conducted by other daring cricketologists. They may inspire you to roll up your sleeves and set up your very own experiment.

—Scrutinize: Could you answer your question with closer observation? For example, if your question was "Do crickets have eyes?" do you think you might be able to find out the answer for yourself by peering at a cricket through a magnifying lens?

—Find an Expert: Do you know a bug expert? Perhaps a local gardener, agricultural advisor, or science teacher can give you a hand. Advice may be only a phone call away.

—Research: Other cricketologists may have already considered and unraveled your question. Maybe the answer lies hidden in a book. It may even be in this one. Turn the page and search through the next section. If that doesn't work, look at some other books or come back to this page and read on.

Can you find three main body sections on this cricket? What parts can you find on each of these sections?

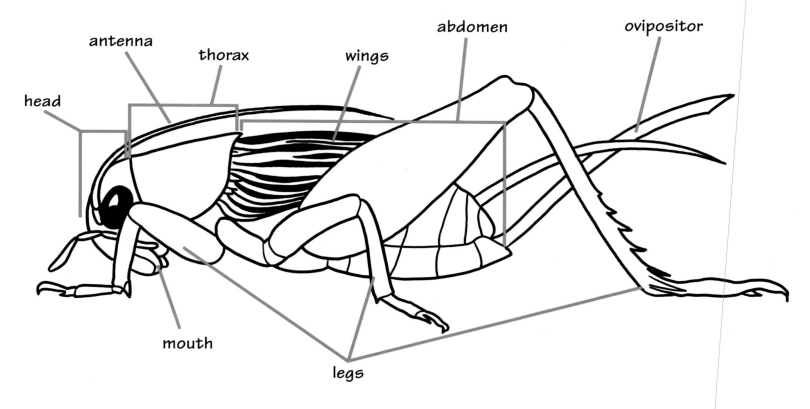

head

antenna

thorax

wings

abdomen

ovipositor

mouth

legs

EXTERNAL CRICKET

Do you have the guts to check out the cricket guts? Peek inside and see if crickets are equipped with some of the same basic parts you are.

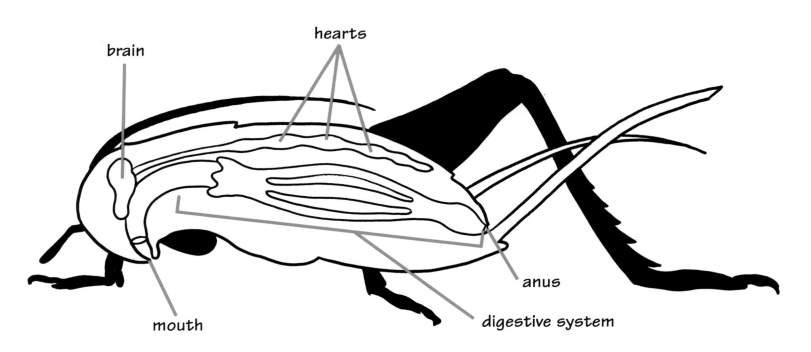

brain

hearts

mouth

anus

digestive system

INTERNAL CRICKET

What hops like a frog? What fights like a rooster? What chirps like a sparrow? What lays eggs like a sea tortoise? Would you believe a cricket?

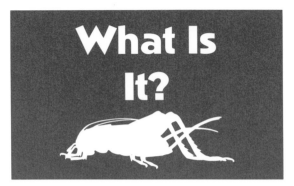

What Is It?

Crickets are part of a group of animals called Orthoptera. Orthoptera are insects. Insects belong to a group of animals called arthropods.

Even though crickets are similar to the above animals, they lack the feathers of a bird, the shell of a tortoise, and the slimy skin of a frog. In fact, a cricket looks more like an ant, bee, beetle, grasshopper, or fly than a bird, reptile, or amphibian. Have you noticed that crickets have three body parts and six legs? Like those of other **insects,** the cricket's body is divided into three body sections: the head, **thorax,** and **abdomen.**

Insects belong to a larger group known as **arthropods.** *Arthro* means "joint" and *pod* means "foot." All arthropods have jointed feet. Centipedes, millipedes, crabs, rolypolies, and spiders are all arthropods and distant cousins of the cricket.

Crickets' closest relatives are the grasshopper, katydid, cockroach, praying mantis, and walking stick. These insects, including the cricket, are part of a smaller group called **Orthoptera** (or-THOP-teh-rah), which means "straight wing."

Examine your cricket and cricket sketches. Does your cricket fit the description of an Orthoptera, an insect, and an arthropod?

Arthropods are creatures with pairs of jointed legs. The animals below are arthropods.

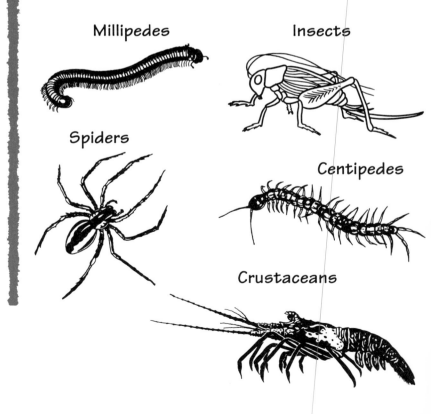

Millipedes

Insects

Spiders

Centipedes

Crustaceans

Insects are arthropods with three body parts and three pairs of legs. The animals below are insects.

Houseflies   Ladybugs   Bees   Crickets   Butterflies

Orthoptera are insects with straight wings. The animals below are orthoptera.

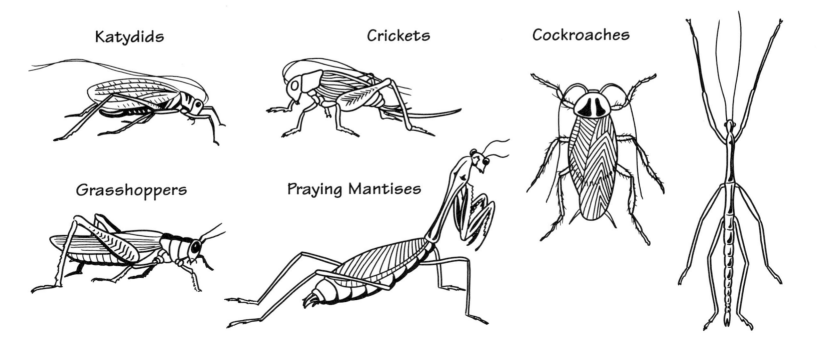

Walkingsticks

Katydids   Crickets   Cockroaches

Grasshoppers   Praying Mantises

Each language has it's own name for crickets. In Hausa, a language of Nigeria, it's *gyàrē,* in Chinese it's *xīshuài,* in Spanish it's *grillo,* and in Dutch it's *krekel.* Having all of these names could be quite mind-boggling to scientists if it weren't for Latin and Greek. Scientists use the ancient languages of Latin and Greek to devise a single name for each living thing. In fact, if you know a little bit about dinosaurs, you already know some scientific names. For example, the word *triceratops,* or "horned dinosaur," comes from the words *tri* (three), *kera* (horn), and *ops* (face). *Acheta domesticus* (AH-kuh-duh deh-MES-tih-kuhs) is the scientific name for the house cricket. *Achet* means "loud singing" and *domus* means "house." Whether you visit a scientist in Nigeria, China, or the Netherlands, each of them will know a cricket by the name *Acheta domesticus.*

Krekel, Grillo . . . Say What?

There are all kinds of crickets. Some species, like house and field crickets, live in our backyards and sometimes even move into our homes. Others, like tree and bush crickets, may be found in neighborhood trees and shrubs. Dressed in white, pale green, or brown, they are often difficult to see as they hide among leaves and stems.

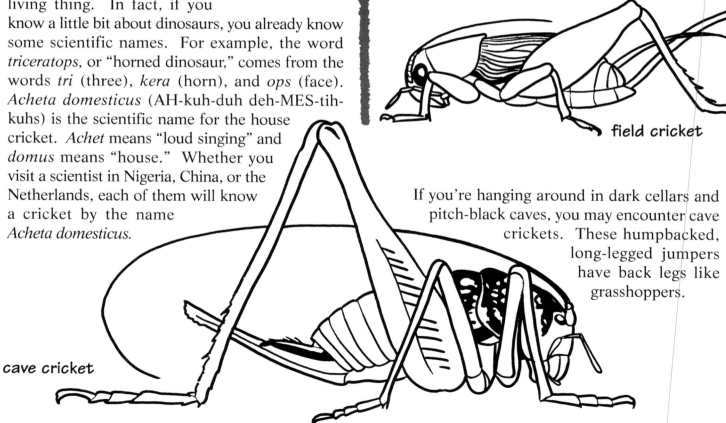

field cricket

cave cricket

If you're hanging around in dark cellars and pitch-black caves, you may encounter cave crickets. These humpbacked, long-legged jumpers have back legs like grasshoppers.

The odd-looking mole cricket burrows under the earth in search of juicy grubs (the wormlike young of certain insects) and sometimes grows as long as your pinkie finger. Like a real mole, the mole cricket has feet shaped like jagged shovels. One type of cricket, found in the eastern United States, lives along with ants in ant colonies. These crickets are as small as the ants they live with.

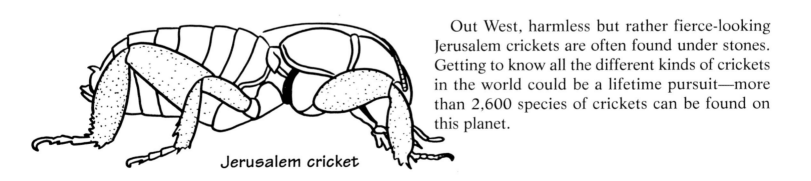

mole cricket

Jerusalem cricket

Out West, harmless but rather fierce-looking Jerusalem crickets are often found under stones. Getting to know all the different kinds of crickets in the world could be a lifetime pursuit—more than 2,600 species of crickets can be found on this planet.

Does your cricket sing? If it does, you are most likely the proud host of a full-grown male cricket. In general, only adult males sing, so if your cricket is quiet, you may have a female or a young male—or an adult male that is too shy to sing. To tell the age and sex of a cricket, simply examine its wings and tail end. An adult field or house cricket has wings that nearly reach the end of its abdomen, while a young cricket, called a **nymph,** may have only wing pads or stubby wings. A female has a long egg-laying tube, called an **ovipositor** (O-veh-PAH-zih-ter), while the male has thick-veined upper wings that look like giant fiddles. Underneath these wings, the male has another pair of wings it uses for flying. Although most crickets can fly, some kinds never actually take off into the air.

Fiddle Wings

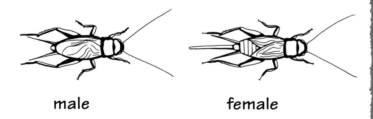

male   female

If you watch a male cricket while it sings, you will notice that it lifts its top wings and holds them over its back. Look closer and you'll see it rubbing one wing over the other. As this happens, the hardened edge of one wing, called the **scraper,** rubs against the ridged part of the other, the **file.** Like the washboard in an old-time band, this produces a buzzing tune.

The faster a cricket rubs its wings, the higher the trill. In 1897, Professor A. E. Dolbear of West Virginia made a remarkable discovery. He had noticed that snowy tree crickets seemed to sing faster on warmer nights. Dolbear came up with a formula for telling the temperature based on the number of chirps heard per minute.

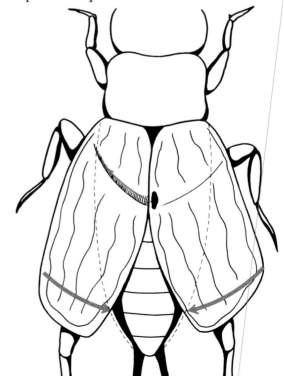

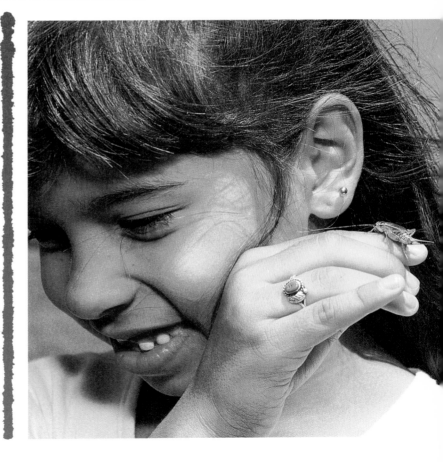

Chirpy Meditation

Though most crickets sing at night, the common field cricket can be heard singing in the daytime too. Place an adult male cricket in your cricket castle and keep it in your bedroom. With a little luck you may be treated to a concert played on one of the Earth's oldest instruments. For millions of years, crickets have been fiddling on their musical wings.

People all over the world celebrate the cricket song. In many parts of Africa, crickets are believed to have magic powers. Listen to your backyard songsters. Tune in to the rhythms. See if you can hear different types of cricket songs. Can you figure out where they are coming from? Consider your mood. Poets picture crickets as merry songsters, symbols of peace, and even sad messengers announcing summer's end. What feelings do you have when listening to cricket songs?

Although people and all other backyard animals are often part of the audience for cricket serenades, these songs are really meant for other crickets. If you have listened carefully to singing crickets, you may have noticed that they sing a variety of songs. The most common tune is the mating call, which can be heard from late spring till early fall. During this mating season, males chirp continually from shallow crevices and burrows in hopes of attracting wandering females of the same species. One European field cricket was recorded chirping 42,000 times in 4 hours and 20 minutes.

Unlike most other animals, crickets wear ears on their elbows. These ears are located on the elbows of their front legs. When a female is ready to select a mate, she faces him with her elbows spread apart. This allows the female to figure out

Elbow Ears

exactly where the male is, just as we do when we turn our heads in trying to discover the source of a sound. Stereo sound receivers, our ears, allow us to focus on the direction of a noise.

When a female field cricket reaches a male, she strokes his **antennae** with hers, so he can sense that she is a female and not a trespassing male. Then the male starts singing a quiet "courtship" song, and mating soon follows.

During mating, females of some species will climb on top of their mates. In this position, the male is able to deliver his **sperm** to a special chamber on the underside of the female's abdomen. To **fertilize** her eggs, or to bring the sperm and egg together so that baby crickets can start growing, all the female has to do is place some sperm in her egg chamber.

Down the Tube

Many people are buried when they die. But how would you like to have been buried before you were born? Or how would you like to hatch from an egg in a tree? Anywhere from a day to a couple of weeks after mating, a female cricket will lay her eggs. Field crickets insert their ovipositors, or egg layers, in soft soil and bury their eggs. Tree crickets lay eggs in tree bark or inside the stems of plants. Neither field nor tree crickets take care of their eggs or young. Mole crickets, on the other hand, build underground burrows where they lay eggs and raise their young.

Newly hatched crickets, or nymphs, look basically like miniature wingless adults. Many other insects, such as butterflies, flies, beetles, and ants, look very different from their parents when they hatch from eggs. These insects hatch as wormlike forms called **larvae** and go through several changes before they become adults. A young cricket doesn't change much before becoming an adult, but it does need to grow. The cricket, like all insects, has a hard outside shell called an **exoskeleton.** Think about how much you grow each year and what would happen if you wore a hard shell. Unless your shell grew, you'd be in trouble. As crickets grow, they shed their too-tight exoskeleton and replace it with a larger one. As a cricket **sheds,** or climbs out of its old shell-like skin, the new layer of skin underneath is already beginning to harden. Shedding occurs 5 to 14 times before crickets reach full size, and after each shedding, the cricket looks a little bit more adult.

Life is not always easy for these young adult crickets. In many parts of the world, winter is so harsh that crickets must seek the protection of a burrow or crevice until spring. The adults of some species of crickets die in the fall and only the young live through winter. In still other species, only the eggs survive to hatch in spring.

On warm quiet evenings as we listen to the hum of cricket song, violent battles may be occuring in our own back-yards. As male crickets sing for females, they are some-times visited by other males looking for safe crevices or burrows to sing from. When a singing cricket notices a trespassing male, it will switch to an "aggressive song" telling the stray male to go away. If the intruder doesn't turn tail and leave, a fight may start. Though fights happen only once in a while in natural settings, they are common among crickets living in crowded conditions.

A cricket fight often begins when one cricket whips the other with its antennae. This is like two people who push and shove before they get down to serious brawling. After the lashing, one of the crickets will usually back off, but if they are both determined to fight, they will raise their upper wings and chirp. Perhaps this is like flexing their muscles.

What follows is some real rough wrestling. As the males grab each other with their front legs, they nip with their sharp jaws. Most fights continue until one fighter is flipped over. Sometimes a leg or antenna is lost, but crickets rarely fight to the death.

Since the Sung Dynasty (A.D. 960–1279), people in China have not only known about cricket fights, they have sponsored championship matches.

Bets are placed and champions are bought for high prices. Tournaments are held in public places or special arenas. Contestants are even divided up into heavy, middle, and lightweight categories, and exceptional fighters are buried in tiny silver coffins when they die.

After the two cricket fighters are set in a special bowl, they try to flee each other. Since they cannot escape, they soon face head to head. To get the crickets excited, the referee whips their antennae with a special brush. Thus irritated, a fight begins. Like ancient battles between enslaved Roman gladiators, the struggles sometimes end in death.

When the English question whether something is right or wrong, they may ask, "Is it cricket?" Romans thought it was okay to force slaves to fight to the death. "Is it cricket" to force animals to fight? Do animals have rights too?

A close look at a cricket's mouthparts will reveal jaws as terrifying as a science fiction monster's, but you can relax. Crickets don't eat people. Instead, crickets chomp on leaves, flowers, fruits, and even other insects, such as termites or **maggots** (the larvae of flies). Most crickets are not picky eaters. By examining the stomach contents of wild crickets, scientists have discovered that they eat pollen, insect eggs, and even cow manure!

Crickets in the laboratory survive on dried pet food, lettuce, and aphids (tiny plant-sucking insects). While most crickets will try just about anything, some do have specialized tastes. One species of beach cricket found in Japan eats only fresh crab meat. It even turns up its antennae at shrimp! Mole crickets, like their namesake the mole, frequently munch earthworms and other small ground-dwelling critters. The wingless, ant-loving cricket dines on perhaps the most interesting food. Living inside ant colonies, these tiny crickets force worker ants to

Backyard Chompers

throw up by tickling their antennae. Then they gobble up this partly digested food that the ants were carrying to young ants.

Crickets themselves are food to many creatures. Lizards, birds, frogs, snakes, skunks, and even cats dine on them. That's why crickets are so quick to find hiding places.

As the young cricketologists at my local elementary school in El Portal, California, explored crickets, they soon found themselves involved in some pretty wild investigations. Equipment and material from the classroom and their homes were used in a variety of fun experiments.

Kid Experiments

ice slows crickets down. Do you agree? Try placing a cricket in a covered bowl inside the fridge (not the freezer!) for a half hour. What happens?

Here's a sample of a few of their scientific adventures in cricketology.

What Happens to Cold Crickets?

Since Allison and Leann live in the mountains where it gets cold in the winter, they were curious about the effect of cold on crickets. Did crickets ever end up on snow or ice? Before placing any crickets on a bed of ice, Allison and Leann decided that they would remove the crickets from the ice immediately if they looked like they were being harmed. They did not want to hurt the crickets.

After setting a cricket on ice cubes inside a plastic container, Leann noticed that the cricket moved slowly and seemed to be eating the ice. Upon closer inspection, she discovered that the cricket was trying to get past one of the ice cubes. When the cold cricket was set in a container without ice cubes, it moved slowly at first, but then tried to climb the walls. The girls concluded that

Can Crickets Learn?

In another experiment, Leann and Allison tested to see if a cricket could find a small escape hole in a container. It took the cricket about five minutes to find the hole, which it then quickly darted through. After being returned to the container, the cricket went straight to the hole again two more times. Leann and Allison thought the cricket remembered where the hole was and that this was a sign of cricket intelligence. What do you think?

Do Crickets Like Light or Dark?

When Jacob bought crickets from bait shops, he noticed that they seemed to cluster around the lightbulb in their cages. "Do they like light?" he wondered. Tylar, Jacob, and GJ devised a testing tube with two equal-length sections of plastic pipe joined with a T fitting. This created one long tube with an opening in the middle. An electric light was placed at one end. Two different crickets were each tested three times by dropping them into the open top of the T fitting. Each time, the boys waited one minute before checking the location of the crickets. Each cricket went to the lighted end two times out of three. The crickets seemed to prefer the light, but the boys had also noticed that the light was warm. Are crickets attracted to heat or light? How could you find out?

How Far Can Crickets Jump?

Cricket jumping was tested on a sidewalk by Caitlin, Chelsea, Libby, and Jessica. They used a yardstick for measuring and fingers for prodding crickets into action. After two crickets jumped five times each, the girls computed the average hop at 9½ inches long.

Would the jumps be farther on different surfaces? After measuring hops on grass, dirt, paper towel, floor tile, and concrete again, the average distances were computed. The results were as follows:

Grass: 6¾ inches
Dirt: 9¼ inches
Concrete: 10¾ inches
Paper towel: 7½ inches
Floor tile: 2 inches

The team of hop investigators decided that tile was too slippery for world-class cricket long jumps, whereas concrete was better because it was rough.

What Will Crickets Eat?

Elizabeth and Melissa served a caged cricket lettuce, orange, and part of a grilled cheese sandwich. After watching the cricket closely for several minutes, Elizabeth noted that the cricket seemed to nibble on the lettuce and orange but left the sandwich alone. Why do you think the crickets stayed away from the grilled cheese sandwich? What else do you think crickets might snack on?

Will Crickets Avoid Snake Scent?

If you have ever picked up a garter snake, you probably have discovered that they stink. Without poisonous venom or sharp fangs, garter snakes defend themselves like skunks. James and Aaron knew that snakes like to eat crickets and wondered if crickets would avoid garter snake odor. After a ball of cotton was rubbed against the class garter snake (kept in a terrarium), it smelled as stinky as the snake. Aaron and James placed the stinky cotton ball on one side of a pan and a normal cotton ball on the opposite side. One at a time, several crickets were placed in the pan. The boys recorded the number of times crickets went near the cotton balls:

Normal Cotton Ball: 5
Stinky Cotton Ball: 3

The boys did not observe any difference in behavior when the crickets approached the cotton balls, so they assumed that the crickets were unaware of the snake odor. They concluded that the crickets couldn't sense the smell because they lack noses. Do you agree?

Can Crickets Swim?

What happens to crickets that fall into ponds or streams? Can they swim? To discover the bathing abilities of crickets, Kim placed several crickets in a bowl of water for one-minute periods. To her surprise, she discovered that they not only stay afloat, but they can also tread water and navigate with ease to the rim of the bowl.

Will Crickets Go in Water?

If a cricket came to a small stream or puddle, would it swim across? Carroll and Jeremy placed a cricket on a dish island in the middle of a baking pan lake. Three times in a row crickets abandoned the island and swam to the lip of the pan where they tried to climb out. Carroll and Jeremy concluded that crickets will definitely take a dive when they are trying to escape.

When you hear crickets chirping, do you think of good, wormless apples? Perhaps you will after tuning in to the experiments of a Canadian cricketologist, L. G. Montheith.

Did you know that the "worms" found in apples are not really worms at all? They are actually maggots, larvae that will change into fruit flies.

After hatching from eggs laid on apples by their mothers, maggots eat their way into the fruit. Apple farmers don't like these maggots, because along with eating the fruit, they spread **bacteria** that cause apples to rot. Many apple farmers use poisonous sprays to rid orchards of these hungry apple munchers.

Since crickets are found in orchards and have been known to eat other insects, L. G. Montheith wondered if orchard crickets ate fruit fly maggots. To find out, he watched crickets in aquarium tanks that were set up like an orchard floor. Rot-

Good Apples

ten apples, apple leaves, and grass clumps were scattered over a layer of soil, and then maggots and crickets were added. After a series of tests using many crickets and maggots, Montheith discovered that crickets ate both rotten apples and maggots. They did not eat apple leaves or grass. Whether maggots were on the surface of the soil, hidden in grass clumps, or burrowed into the soil, the crickets found and dined on them.

Since the apples that fall on the ground supply crickets with food and good hiding places, Montheith was not surprised when he counted more crickets in orchards where fallen apples were left on the ground. Because more crickets mean fewer maggots, he decided that leaving apples on the ground makes it less necessary for farmers to control apple maggots with dangerous pesticides. Funny as it seems, a messy orchard full of cricket song and rotten apples may be a better place for growing wormless apples.

When Andrea Schatral, a cricketologist from Australia, learned from other scientists that female bush crickets usually picked the largest male bush crickets as mates, she wondered if it had anything to with their songs. Did the females find the biggest male crickets because they had different voices than smaller ones?

Schatral collected 35 mating male crickets and 35 of their nearest nonmating male neighbors in the Australian bush. Back in her laboratory, she measured the crickets and discovered that most of the mating males were larger than their neighbors. She then recorded their songs and analyzed their voices. It turned out that in most cases the mating males had lower voices than their unmated neighbors.

But Shatral couldn't figure out for sure how the females ended up with the bigger, deeper-voiced males. Did the females choose the males based on their voices? Did the bigger males scare away smaller males with their deep-voiced

songs? Did the males choose the females? Like most curious scientists, Andrea Schatral ended her study with more questions for fellow explorers to chew on.

Although this is the end of the book, it is only the beginning of cricketology. Remember those cricket questions you jotted down? Did you find answers to any of them? This book might not be big enough to answer everyone's cricket ponderings. Perhaps there are too many cricket questions to be answered by any book. Maybe no one has even pursued your question before. It could be up to you to search for an answer!

While easily answered questions are like unwrapped presents, tangled mysteries are buried

treasure. Unanswered questions are often more interesting and exciting to scientists than the questions that have answers. Buried treasure questions can lead to new discoveries—and even more new questions. Think about your mysterious questions once more and imagine the explorations they could take you on. Pick up a shovel and dig at those questions.

Below are some buried treasure questions that kids from El Portal may still be excavating at this very moment.

Why do crickets rest together?

Why are their back legs yellow underneath?

Why do they each have a red dot on their foreheads?

Why are crickets black?

What leftover questions do you have?

Glossary

abdomen: the rear section of an insect's body

antennae: sense organs found in pairs on the heads of certain animals, such as insects

arthropods: a group of animals that lacks backbones, has bodies in sections, and has joined feet

bacteria: tiny, one-celled animals, some of which cause disease

exoskeleton: a hard outer shell that supports an animal's body like a skeleton

fertilize: the coming together of sperm and egg to create new life

file: the ridged underside of a cricket's wing that produces sound when rubbed by the scraper on the other wing

grubs: the wormlike larvae, or young, of some insects

insect: an arthropod with six legs and three body sections

larvae: the wormlike stage in the growth of some insects

maggots: the legless larvae, or young, of flies

Orthoptera: a group of straight-winged insects that includes grasshoppers, crickets, katydids, and locusts

ovipositor: an egg-laying tube found on some female insects, such as crickets

scraper: the edge of a cricket's wing that rubs against the file of the other wing, producing sound

shed: to peel off an outer shell or a layer of skin

species: a group of animals with common traits, especially the means of creating young

sperm: the fluid males make to fertilize a female's eggs

thorax: the middle section of an insect, where legs and wings are attached

Index

About the Author

For the last twenty years, Michael Elsohn Ross has taught visitors to Yosemite National Park about the park's wildlife and geology. Mr. Ross, his wife, Lisa (a nurse who served nine seasons as a ranger-naturalist), and their son, Nick, have led other families on wilderness expeditions from the time Nick learned to crawl. Mr. Ross studied conservation of natural resources at the University of California/Berkeley, with a minor in entomology (the study of insects). He spent one summer at Berkeley raising thousands of red-humped caterpillars and parasitic wasps for experiments.

Mr. Ross makes his home on a bluff above the wild and scenic Merced River, at the entrance to Yosemite. His backyard garden is a haven for rolypolies, crickets, snails, slugs, worms, and a myriad of other intriguing critters.